School Impr
Planning Made
Guide for School Leaders and Subject Leaders

by

Jill C Foster

ISBN: 978-1-916820-73-9

Acknowledgements

First and foremost, I am profoundly grateful to the countless teachers, school leaders, CEOs, and policymakers who pour their hearts into building a brighter future through education. It is your wisdom, passion, and insights from the frontlines that breathe life into these words. This book is but a small tribute to your resilience and dedication.

I am indebted to David Smith, CEO of Silicon Valley High School, for first opening my eyes to the vast potential of artificial intelligence to transform learning. Your provocative insights planted the seed that grew into this journey.

To my friend and mentor Dene Lindley, your guidance through my first steps as a writer was invaluable. Thank you for selflessly giving your time and expertise to nurture my growth as an author. Thank you for your wisdom and encouragement.

A special thanks to Debbie Secker and Vicky Fenton for providing crucial perspective from the classroom and the educational sector. Your honest insights and feedback were instrumental in shaping the ideas presented here.

To my incredibly supportive husband Dave, thank you for enduring my AI obsession these past months with patience and humour. I'm grateful every day for your unconditional love and support. You are my best friend.

To my family, I am blessed with a wonderful family who fill my life with joy. Your pride in my work means the world to me.

I am grateful to Anthropic for granting permission to use excerpts of conversations with their artificial intelligence Claude throughout the book. Claude's unique Constitutional AI architecture made the AI–human collaboration presented here possible.

Thank you also to the Education Endowment Foundation for allowing me to reference their invaluable Implementation Guidance resources. The EEF's evidence-based approach served as a guiding light in developing the frameworks presented.

Finally, to the visionaries driving innovations in artificial intelligence – please continue advancing this technology with the utmost care and concern for humanity. Work closely with educators to guide your efforts. The future is unfolding rapidly, and our children's lives hang in the balance. Progress responsibly.

Biography

Jill Foster is a director of Janus Education Ltd, an educational consultancy company that provides advice and support to schools and educators. She is also a co-founder of Secure Schools, a cyber security company specialising in the education sector.

Jill has a wealth of experience, having spent 39 years as a teacher, leader, and innovator. She was the founding CEO of the Rose Learning Trust, a multi-academy trust that operates in England. She has also contributed to educational research and publishing, having authored a CollectEd paper.

Jill is passionate about education and its impact on society. She continues to shape school strategy and improvement through evidence-based practices and technology. Her goal is to make a positive difference in the lives of pupils and educators in our schools.

Contents

Tools I used to write this book (aside from Claude AI) Bing: https://www.bing.com/.

Introduction

Unlock a New Era of AI-Powered Planning in Schools

As a subject leader or senior leader working in school, immense dedication and care is required to create meaningful improvement in your subject and/or school. We pour over data, research best practices, and make difficult yet wise decisions to put pupils/students at the forefront of our decision making. This time-consuming process contributes to us all feeling time poor.

But what if we could amplify our expertise with cutting-edge technology?

Are you ready to discover the power of artificial intelligence? Join me on a journey to explore how AI can revolutionise the way we work. By ethically harnessing AI, we can streamline tedious tasks and free up valuable time. Guided by The EEF Implementation Guidance 2019 (1), we'll learn how to create clear, logical implementation plans focused on the active ingredients – the essential components that make the practice work. Don't miss out on this opportunity to discover a new paradigm. Join me and let's explore the possibilities together.

Educationalists want to engage with research, but where to start? Using the detailed prompts, you can analyse information, access and quality assure suggested research, and use your professional judgement and expertise to finalise and create implementation plans in a fraction of the time.

The book is organised into two main parts:

Part 1: AI-Powered School Improvement Planning: A Practical Blueprint and Guide.

Part 2: Deepening Your Knowledge and Understanding of AI.

Prompt Templates Access: A bank of downloadable sample prompts are also provided on purchase of the book so you can simply cut and paste the prompts.

Part 1

AI-Powered School Improvement Planning: A Practical Blueprint and Guide

Chapter 1

Choosing the Optimal AI Assistant for Education Leaders

Education leaders and subject leaders have a useful option in chatbot AI, which enables natural conversations using normal written language. Intelligent chatbots can be valuable aids, though they lack human-level discernment. Used appropriately, they support leaders in leveraging AI efficiency while retaining education's humanity.

From personal experience, I have found the Claude chatbot well-suited for leadership tasks. Created by Anthropic using Constitutional AI for human value alignment, Claude summarises texts concisely, gives honest responses if knowledge is lacking, and has a key training cutoff date in 2023. This recent training provides an advantage in conversing about current educational research and events.

Anthropic has a deep commitment to AI safety. Trained on Constitutional AI, they aim to create helpful AI systems while avoiding unintended harm by following safety principles drawn from sources like the Universal Declaration of Human Rights.

This ethical approach was an important consideration for me working in the education sector and with my background in educational cyber security; however, other chatbots may be used in a similar way. It is a personal choice for you to make.

When selecting an AI provider, be sure to investigate their data privacy and protection policies, and opt for services that encrypt data, allow opting out of storing conversations, and provide transparency around how your data may be used. Establish clear internal guidelines on appropriate usage and consider your school's policy toward using AI.

If you decide to use Claude, which is currently free, I have outlined how this can be done below:

Accessing Anthropic's Claude AI

Getting access is quick and easy.

- Go to the Claude website at claude.ai.
- Click "Get Started" and then "Join the waitlist" to sign up with your email address.
- You will be emailed an access code once it is your turn to create an account.
- Return to the Claude website and click "Activate account" on the homepage.
- Enter the emailed access code and create a password to set up your account.
- You can then log in any time with your email and password by clicking "Log in" at the top right of the Claude homepage.
- Start by clicking the chat icon on the left to open the chat interface. Introduce yourself to Claude and explain you are a school leader exploring its capabilities. Claude will greet you and ask clarifying questions to understand your role and needs.

While chatting with Claude, you can star or bookmark particularly helpful responses under your chat history.

Don't forget to provide Claude feedback on its responses so it continues improving.

Troubleshooting Tips for Claude:

- If conversations are slow, try smaller attachments under 10MB: large files strain the interface.
- Restart chat if experiencing errors uploading attachments or text gaps. Connectivity issues occasionally occur.
- If Claude seems stuck in a repetitive loop, end chat and start afresh. This usually resolves any glitches.
- For continued issues, contact Claude's customer support who are quite responsive to technical issues.

As a special bonus for buying the book, I'm pleased to provide you with exclusive access to my proprietary prompt templates for school improvement planning. These prompts encapsulate many man hours in distilling key educational challenges and goals into optimised AI conversations.

While the prompts represent my intellectual property developed specifically for this book, I'm excited to share them with you as a valued reader. I trust you will find them hugely helpful in streamlining your own planning.

Please note that to retain the value of these resources for you as a buyer of the book, I'm requesting that you do not share the prompt templates or this download link with anyone else who has not purchased their own copy of the book. My ability to continue providing these assets relies on your discretion.

I hope you obtain immense value from these exclusive prompts. Thank you again for supporting my work – it means the world to me. I wish you the very best as you integrate AI into your improvement planning!

All the prompts can be found here.

https://www.dropbox.com/scl/fi/jld2fe8mv1a5hxlpjbqc9/Prompt-Sharing.docx?rlkey=dw9e78yflti1ut0ucw0v4j6ft&dl=0

As educationalists we want to ensure that Claude is transparent about any limitations.

Prompt 1 – type this into the chat box:

> **Acting as my educational assistant*School data analyst*School implementation planner*What are your limitations when assisting me as a school leader* ***and/or*** *subject leader?*

It is important to note that the examples provided in this book are based on the AI model's knowledge and capabilities at the time of writing. As AI evolves and learns more, examples of AI chat may change.

> Claude's Response at the time of writing:
>
> "As an AI assistant created by Anthropic to be helpful, harmless, and honest, I have some important limitations

to be transparent about when supporting you as a school leader:

- I do not actually have access to real data about your specific school or students. I can only work with the information you provide to me. Any data analysis or planning I assist with will be limited without genuine insights into your specific school community.

- My knowledge comes from public information and training by Anthropic. I do not have human experiences like working in schools or as an education professional. You will need to interpret my suggestions through the lens of your practical expertise.

- While I can generate ideas and content, I lack discernment to make nuanced judgements. Any plans or suggestions I offer should be carefully reviewed.

- There may be errors or biases in my responses based on limitations in my training data and statistical models. Please verify any facts or data I provide.

- I do not have a full understanding of important contextual factors like school cultures, teacher dynamics, student needs etc. My advice will be generic unless you provide specific local context.

- As an AI system, I do not actually have personal educational experiences or qualifications. I cannot replace the wisdom gained from years as an education practitioner.

- I am unable to make final decisions on plans. My role should be assisting human leaders who remain accountable.

- I lack emotional intelligence and the ability to form meaningful relationships with students, teachers, and communities. This human connection is essential in education.

In summary, I can provide information and ideas as an aid, but lack real-world experience. My value is in assisting professionals like you, not replacing them. Please let me know if I can explain my capabilities and limitations further! I hope to be helpful while keeping realistic expectations."

As you can see for Claude's response there are clear limitations on how Claude can assist you. We want to make this clear from the start of this guide. AI cannot do the entire job of implementation planning for you. I would like to reinforce what Claude's output said:

"I am unable to make final decisions on plans. My role should be assisting human leaders who remain accountable."

AI systems such as Claude have boundaries on knowledge that may sometimes result in incorrect responses. The AI confident responses may lead readers to accept the information as a given. This does not represent an intention to deceive on the part of AI. Any inaccuracies simply reflect current technical limitations. As the user of AI, use your human discernment and wisdom. Also please refer to the chapter "AI Hallucinations" later in the book.

I encourage you to think critically about the information provided, and double check any facts, references, or quotes. The role of AI is to offer information to assist you, not serve as an infallible source of absolute truth. By working together, communicating openly, and verifying details, you can help strengthen Claude's (or any other chatbot's) capabilities over time while fully leveraging your own human intellect and insight.

Prompt 2 – type this into the chat box using your own name:

**Act as my personal educational assistant*data analyst*educational researcher*and implementation planner*please indicate if your suggestions require validating with:*

"Hypothesised data" if lacking the school's real internal data.

"External benchmarking" if extrapolating trends without up-to-date national/regional data

"Assumption checking" if based on unverified premises.

"Fact-checking" if providing detailed statistics.

"Research findings" if proposing teaching strategies lacking citations or evidence.

"My goal is an implementation plan grounded in reality and proven methods. Please flag areas needing more

factual confirmation or educational research so I can verify them. Please seek clarification if you are unsure what requires validating. Concise flags help me assess where to dig deeper."

The main focuses are:

- Flag hypothetical data without school insights

- Note extrapolations needing external benchmark comparison

- Highlight assumptions requiring checking

- Indicate statistics requiring fact checking

- Cite research backing suggested approaches

Claude's response will be transparent about its limitations.

You will notice during chat 1 and 2 that Claude automatically uses US spelling. I have included below another prompt that you can use to address this if you work in the UK sector:

Your Prompt 3 – Type the following into Claude's chat box:

Prompt:

Claude, your response to all my chats will use UK spelling. ***As a user from a country where standard UK spelling is commonly used, I prefer to communicate using* *this spelling convention. To ensure consistency and clarity in our communication, please respond to all chats using standard UK spelling. This includes using standard UK spellings for words such as "colour", "favourite", "centre", and "defence", "personalised" and "utilise" instead of the standard US spellings "color", "favorite", "center", "defense", personalize" and "utilize".*If you are unsure of the correct spelling for a word, please consult a reliable dictionary or reference source that uses standard UK spelling.*Indicate to me if there are grey areas**

This was Claude's response:

"Thank you for the clear guidance. I will be happy to use standard UK spelling in all my responses going forward. Please let me know if I incorrectly use any Americanised spellings, and I will promptly correct them. I appreciate you taking the time to provide this context, as it will allow us to communicate smoothly using your preferred conventions. I look forward to continuing our conversations using standard UK spelling."

Claude will adhere to using standard UK spelling in all chats going forward. You do not need to repeat this prompt every time you start a new conversation.

Chapter 2

Build Your Plan on the EEF's Proven Implementation Framework

The Education Endowment Fund (EEF) provides a structured approach to evidence-based implementation planning: **"Putting Evidence to Work: A School's Guide to Implementation Guidance Report 2019"**. (1) The EEF approach is utilised in this handbook. This is a highly recommended guidance document that I urge you to read fully, using this link:

https://educationendowmentfoundation.org.uk/education-evidence/guidance-reports/implementation

Here you can find the Guidance Report/Recommendation Poster and additional tools. You will also find sample implementation plans as well as the EEF planning template, which you will need in the next chapter.

As this is a handbook, I have provided a summary of the guidance key points:

- Implementation is a **process** that happens in stages over an extended period. It involves thinking about, preparing for, delivering, and sustaining change.
- Schools should allow enough time for each stage, particularly preparation.
- School leadership and climate are foundations for good implementation. Leaders should create a vision, set expectations, build capacity through teams, and identify implementation leaders. The school climate should empower staff to try new things.
- When selecting a practice to implement, leaders should build a rich evidence picture, look beyond surface details, and focus on the *"How"* of implementation not just the *"What"*. Leaders should integrate **research evidence with professional judgement**.
- Leaders should create a clear, logical implementation plan focused on the active ingredients – the essential components that make the practice work. Develop appropriate implementation strategies and define outcomes to monitor.
- Assess readiness to deliver the plan. Once ready, prepare through training, follow-on coaching, peer collaboration, and developing the infrastructure.
- Support staff during initial delivery through flexible leadership, expert coaching, using data, and making thoughtful adaptations.

- Plan for sustaining and scaling the practice from the outset. Treat scale-up as a new implementation process. Continuously acknowledge and reward good practices.

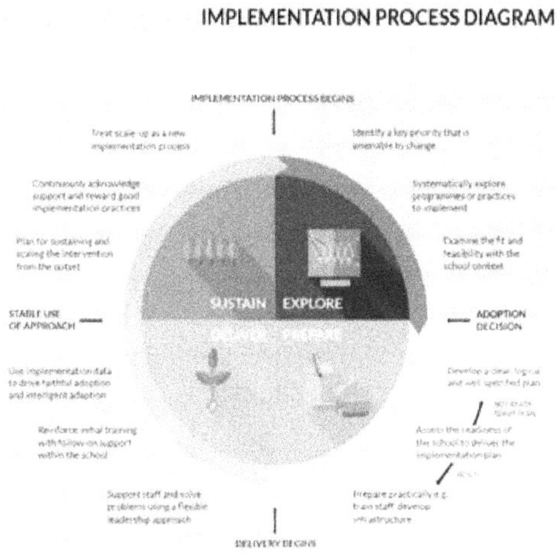

Figure 1: Implementation can be described as a series of stages relating to thinking about, preparing for, delivering and sustaining change.

In this guide I will share with you educationally designed prompts to take you through each stage of implementation: **explore, prepare, deliver and sustain.**

This guide will take you through:

- An **exploration exercise** with Claude to explore hard and soft data from your school to enable you to summarise the root problem you are addressing in your plan and establish specific goals with Claude's help.

- Looking at **research-informed solutions**, programmes and strategies which you can filter and add to your own current exploration solutions.
- Creating a **draft implementation plan** which through the complex prompting allows you to:

-Follow a consistent structure addressing the problem, intervention ingredients, implementation activities, outcomes, and impact.

-Contains a problem statement which is informed by analysing school data to identify specific student/teacher needs.

-Contain active ingredients emphasising evidence-based approaches tailored to the needs of the students.

-Include implementation activities which provide practical details on training, coaching, resources, monitoring, and communication which need to be carried out.

-Include outcomes with measurable targets related to fidelity, reach, and acceptability.

-Focus on tangible improvements in student engagement, skills, and attainment.

Overarching Theme				
Problem (Why)	Intervention Description (What?) Active Ingredients	Implementation Activities (How)	Implementation Outcomes short, medium and long term (How well?)	Final outcomes (And so?)

- Creating a **delivery plan**.
- Creating a **sustainability plan**.
- Creating a **Monitoring and Evaluation plan**.

My aim is to provide a model for connecting evidence-based interventions to practical applications in schools through supported, monitored, and adjustable approaches. The level of detail they contain provides actionable steps while keeping the focus on measurable student impact.

You may be familiar with the exemplars that are on the EEF website. This is how an implementation plan should look when complete.

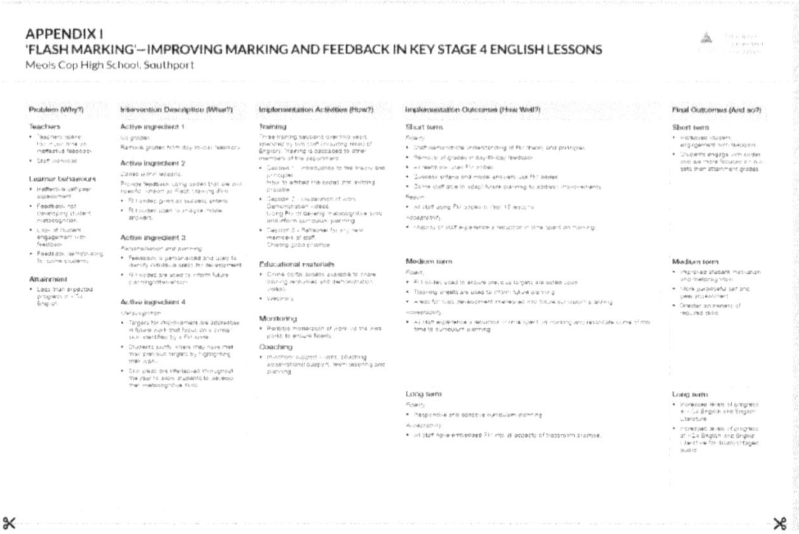

APPENDIX I
'FLASH MARKING'—IMPROVING MARKING AND FEEDBACK IN KEY STAGE 4 ENGLISH LESSONS
Meols Cop High School, Southport

Problem (Why?)	Intervention Description (What?)	Implementation Activities (How?)	Implementation Outcomes (How Well?)	Final Outcomes (And so?)
Teachers; Learner behaviours; Attainment	Active ingredient 1; Active ingredient 2; Active ingredient 3; Active ingredient 4	Training; Educational materials; Monitoring; Coaching	Short term; Medium term; Long term	Short term; Medium term; Long term

EEF Exemplar Implementation Plans (2)

Be sure to download the full EEF guidance report as it provides invaluable recommendations impossible to fully capture here. Use it as an ongoing reference while planning.

Priming Claude

To ensure that Claude is fully up-to-date with the EEF guidance I am going to download two documents directly into Claude's chat box:

1. The EEF Implementation Guidance 2019
2. The examples of implementation plans from the EEF website.

Download the EEF Implementation Guidance first so that the document appears in the chat as below. You are now ready to prompt Claude:

Prompt 4 – Type the following into Claude's chat box:

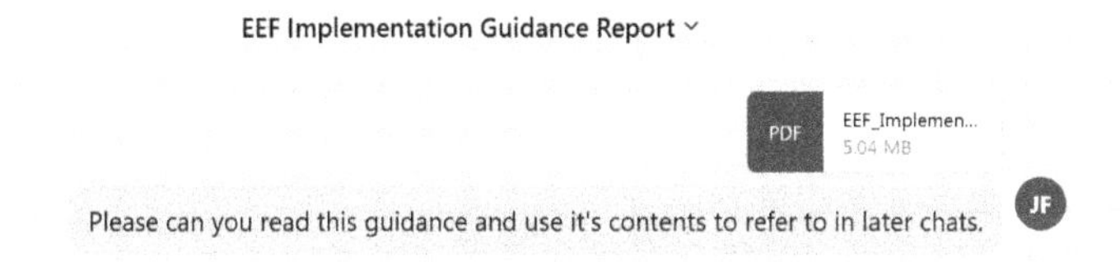

When priming Claude, speak conversationally as you would to a colleague. For example, "Let's look at this EEF implementation excerpt together" rather than "Upload resource for assistant to process."

Prompt 5 – Type the following into Claude's Chat Box:

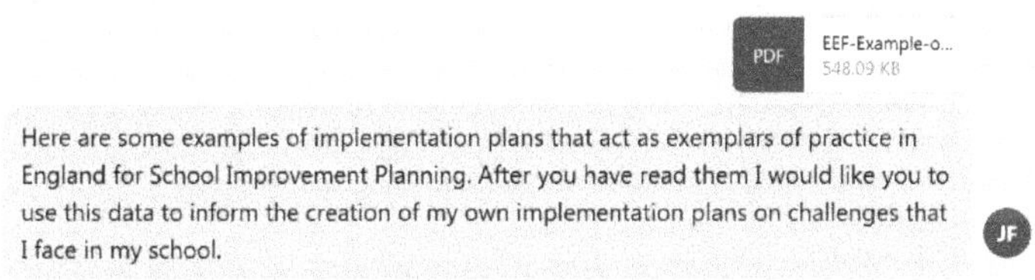

Here is the link to the PDF: https://d2tic4wvo1iusb.cloudfront.net/production/eef-guidance-reports/implementation/EEF-Example-of-Implementation-Plans.pdf?v=1692705886

Claude now has this information that you can call on later from your own library.

I urge you to spend time considering priming. What recent documents are available to help Claude deepen its knowledge on the domain of your implementation plan?

You could consider the following sources:

- DfE guidance.
- EEF website tools/guidance.
- Ofsted subject reviews.
- Chartered College research.
- Selected text that can deepen and strengthen Claude's understanding of the problem area.

Chapter 3

Streamline Planning with AI-Generated Implementation Blueprints

Screenshots of conversations with Anthropic's Claude are included in this book with permission from Anthropic. The Education Endowment Fund have also granted permission to reference their Implementation Guidance 2019. Sample AI outputs have not been added to this chapter as they may contain references to educational approaches or proprietary content, of which permission has not been granted.

To model the production of an implementation plan with Claude I have selected a common problem in practice in any phase of education, oracy, language, and vocabulary development.

This is a common problem which many schools are addressing in the aftermath of Covid.

A key finding from Speech and Language UK (2022) Speaking Up for the Covid Generation was that: "1.5 million children are at risk of not being able to speak or understand language at an age-appropriate level."

Please note that while AI can provide valuable support, it is not a substitute for professional educators. Its role is to **assist and provide information**, just like a PA, but the successful execution of the plan ultimately relies on the expertise and commitment of the school staff and stakeholders. This includes the checking of the data that

Claude provides, just as you would if a PA presented ideas as to how you might complete a task on your behalf. . The practiced educationalist would select and check the information to "Explore" the information and check that this is fit for purpose.

To create an implementation plan we will create a super prompt in three different stages. These are the **three steps to success:**

Step 1 – Data exploration with Claude acting as a prompt engineer.

Step 2 – Exploring research and best practice with Claude generating appropriate activities related to your problem that you can evaluate and select for use.

Step 3 – Planning using Claude as a master implementation plan generator.

- **Open a new chat with Claude and <u>stay</u> in the same chat for <u>all three steps.</u>**

Claude will only act on what you prompt. So human input is needed to ensure that the final prompt is as accurate as possible and can be contextual to your school.

Step 1. Data Exploration

As an educator focusing on pedagogy rather than technology, I am not claiming to have expertise in the technical details of prompt engineering. However, through experience I have found that careful prompting can greatly enhance communication with AI systems like Claude. The prompts I provide are formulated based on principles of effective communication – being specific about intent, clearly stating desired output and using UK spelling.

Though I am not a computer scientist, the prompts I design have proven successful in reducing workload considerably by delegating appropriate tasks to Claude. Prompting is like conducting an orchestra, with each component playing a role in achieving the desired outcome.

My role is to provide prompts from an educational perspective. This is the domain of my experience, to elicit Claude's capabilities in a pedagogically sound manner. I am sure those with advanced technical expertise in prompt engineering and AI will see room for improvement; however, a prompt engineer may not understand some of the probing questions that can be employed to provoke deep thought in subject leaders and senior leaders alike.

My focus in sharing these prompts with you is leveraging Claude's skills through thoughtful prompting to enhance the learning experience, not on training Claude itself. I leave the finer technical points of prompt optimisation to the computer scientists and hope to collaborate to continuously refine prompts that bring out the best in AI for education.

Exploring data to seek out the root of the problem.

Prompt 6 – Type the following into Claude's chat box (yes, it's very complex, but that is what gets the results). Please cut and paste the prompt from the link I have provided and individualise the red text to your own context:

***Prompt me to have a collaborative discussion with you, Claude, to identify key data sources that reveal an oral language gap among students and determine focused goals for improvement.**

**Context* Oral language skills provide the vital foundation for academic success. Students proficient in vocabulary, listening comprehension, and verbal expression are primed to excel. However, many students enter school lacking these critical skills, facing an oral language gap that widens over time.

** Framing the Discussion* Let's have an insightful discussion to dig into the data that demonstrates this gap and determine strategic improvement goals. You'll guide me with probing questions to:*

**Analyse national and internal assessment data trends over time. Do these reveal an oral language gap? Which skills are lagging?*

**Pinpoint the student groups most disproportionately affected. What factors contribute to their struggles?*

**Articulate the real-world benefits if we can successfully boost students' oral language abilities. How will this set them up for academic and lifelong success?*

*Establish 3–4 focused, incremental oral language goals and metrics to close this gap. For example: should we aim for 75% proficiency by Year 3, and 100% by Year 6?

Key Sources to Analyse Let's do a deep dive on insights from:

*National Early Years Foundation Stage Profile and Key Stage 1/2 data/KS3/GCSE.

*Internal tracking and teacher observations of vocabulary, listening, and verbal expression.

*Interviews and surveys gathering staff, parent, and student perspectives.

*External feedback such as Ofsted TFIs.

Guiding Questions

-"What root causes may be contributing to the oral language gap?"

-"Which student groups are most affected and why?"

-"What are the real-world benefits if we can successfully boost oral language skills?"

_"What specific, measurable goals make sense based on the data trends?"

_Outcome*–Our goal is to summarise key data insights, produce an **overarching title statement** for an implementation plan, and **establish 3–4 focused oral language goals** with metrics.*Please respond in UK English **

Simply type this prompt into the chat box and away you go. Answer Claude's prompts with your own school problem and data, or you can use mine to try the process out quickly for yourself.

For my fictional primary school, I will respond to Claude's prompts using the following data when asked.

Fictional data for Cherry Tree Primary School which I will share with Claude:

- The focus is to improve spoken language across the school so that students leave at Y6 with vocabulary and language at an age-appropriate level. I want to progressively diminish the current vocabulary gap in Cherry Tree Lane Primary School.
- The school is larger than national average with 450 pupils. The school has a high level of disadvantage: 43% of pupils are pupil premium.
- Baseline EYFS data suggests that EYFS pupils arrive in school with underdeveloped speech and poor vocabulary: 60% of pupils entering at EYFS baseline with below expected oral language skills.
- 25% have identified speech/language needs.
- Language and vocabulary are negatively impacting on reading and writing. KS1 and KS2 outcomes lag national averages.
- Ofsted highlighted speech/language/vocabulary as an area for improvement at the last inspection.
- Some students lack foundational skills like nursery rhymes and book engagement when entering school.
- Quality student interactions are infrequent with some pupils on entry, and language gaps persist into Y6.
- PD so far has focused on teachers more than teaching assistants.
- Parent engagement has so far not addressed language or vocabulary development.
- Staff lack confidence in meeting language learning needs in the classroom.
- Observations in the classroom have provided data that suggests pupils of tier 2 and tier 3 vocabulary need development to support reading and language comprehension.

- Subject leaders of some subjects have not paid sufficient attention to developing vocabulary and encouraging talk.
- Data suggests 20% of homes do not have access to many books.
- Some pupils enter EYFS still using pacifiers.
- Some pupils access long periods of screen time
- The pupil premium strategy has identified speech, language, and vocabulary development as a challenge for the most disadvantaged pupils in the school.
- 25% of pupils have speech, language, and communication as a primary need; this rises to 30% in SEND pupils.
- Staff reflective practice is not evident and could be greatly improved.
- I want to concentrate on accelerated focus on EYFS to get 50% of pupils to expected levels by Y1. The goal is to reach 70% by Y2 and fully eradicate the gap by Y6 with 100% at expected level for vocabulary and oracy.
- There is no tracking of oracy or vocabulary currently. Any tracking and assessment must impact positively on pupils, but I am mindful of staff work–life balance. Any assessment must be swift, easy, and actionable.
- Identification of speech, language and communication needs is inconsistent.
- There are inconsistencies in staff approaches in class to speech, language, and communication as well as vocabulary in classroom.
- There are no speech and language interventions.
- Infrequent active conversations in early childhood have been identified as a contributing factor to the vocabulary issue.

Claude will build up an understanding of the problems you want to address, as well as suggest potential measurable goals.

Claude and I summarised the problems and issues at Cherry Tree Lane Primary as:

Claude's response:

Overarching Title Statement:
Bridging the Oral Language Gap: A Strategic Plan to Accelerate Vocabulary, Listening, and Verbal Skills for Academic Success

Goals and Metrics:
1. Improve receptive and expressive vocabulary skills, with students reaching expected levels for their age
- 50% of EYFS/KS1 students at age- expected oral language level by Year 1
- 70% of EYFS/KS1 students at age-expected oral language level by Year 2
- 100% of students at age-expected oral language level by Year 6

2. Increase meaningful student interactions and discussions across all year levels
- Implement daily partner and small group discussions in every classroom
- Require open-ended questioning and conversation prompts for all subjects

3. Provide early identification and intervention for speech/language needs
- Screen all EYFS students within first month of school
- Develop tailored interventions for students not reaching expected language levels

4. Equip staff with training and resources to integrate oral language development across the curriculum
- 90% of teachers report increased confidence in oral language instructional strategies
- Observations show vocabulary and discussion integrated in 90% of lessons

Step 2 – Exploring the Research

Prompt 7 – Type the following into Claude's chat box:

"Act as my **Educational Researcher: your aim is to identify research-based approaches, schemes and interventions that are tailored to address the key problems/goals that have been identified as:

Copy and paste your problem and goals here from stage 1 →

that you have copied into your own document.

*Your output should be 7–8 specific approaches, **schemes, or interventions** that have evidence to show that they have positively impacted on improving the problem/goals identified*The output should be detailed with sufficient information to the reader to understand the approach without a word limit:

-Focus on pedagogical approaches, policies, and curriculum.

-Provide the research source information in bold, including author(s), year published.

-Briefly explain how implementing this approach could positively impact the specific problems at my school.

-Focus on recent research (past 5 years) using academic journals and reports, EEF toolkit, EEF guidance and documents I have uploaded into your library.

-Be presented as a summary on each approach which is sufficiently detailed to allow me to fully understand the approaches * at least 500 words.

-There is no page or word limit for your responses. I want sufficient detail to understand the programme or approach you are presenting.

-Output should be in UK English.

-Provide an accurate explanation of where each piece of research can be found including the URL so that I can swiftly fact check it.

Claude will give you a range of research-based approaches that you can select from or add to if you already have an approach in mind.

Prompting

Prompting takes time to master. That's why the prompts have been generated for you in Part 1 to help create your implementation plan with ease of effort. The prompting section in Part 2 will allow you to experiment with developing your own prompts that deliver results.

You will have to read and choose the approaches from Claude's selection and maybe add some of your own.

You as the author of your plan have the sole authority to copy and paste the exact approaches you want to include in your plan into the next prompt that you, the human, have strategically selected for your school, context, and community.

As with any assistant, it is the author's responsibility to check authenticity and validity.

Personally, I would always advocate that at this stage you ask Claude for more detail and information on specific research which you may use in your plan. Let Claude make your fact checking easier by continuing the prompting as many times as you see fit. Once you are satisfied with this stage, we can move on to the implementation plan itself. I have used the EEF Implementation Guidance 2019 to guide my prompt.

Step 3 – Creating the Draft Implementation Plan Ready for you to Quality Assure

Prompt 8 – Type the following into Claude's chat box:

*"Act as an **Expert School Implementation Plan Generator*** to develop an accessible, clear, and focused implementation plan of approximately 2500 words.* The implementation activities will warrant more text.

*Begin with a 1-paragraph executive summary briefly introducing the plan.

*The full plan should address the key problems and goals.

➡ Place the problem you defined in step 1.

Follow this format:

*Overarching Theme: A succinct, descriptive title summarising the plan's focus.

***The Problem**: Clearly explain core problems this plan will address under sub-headings for students, staff, and student outcomes/achievement.

***Intervention Description**: Describe all major interventions/initiatives to address the problems. For each, state the active ingredients needed for successful implementation in bold. Active ingredients should include necessary staff professional development in preparation, delivery, and sustainability of the intervention.

***Implementation Activities**: Provide detailed activities involved in rolling out the interventions, explaining the rationale grounded in research (cited in smaller font)

***Implementation Outcomes**: Define specific short, medium, and long-term outcomes with measurable targets related to the goals, using small, measurable, achievable, realistic, and timed (SMART) formats where possible.

1. Final Expected Outcomes: Summarise the **expected impact** on pupil gains and progress if implementation is successful.
2. Integrate specific activities underpinned by research in the active ingredient section.

➡ **Place selected research you want to use in your plan from step 2 here.**

3. Ensure that the output contains sufficient detail to inform the reader, ensuring that there is detail around the active ingredients and implementation activities.
4. Integrate insights from the EEF implementation guidance on specifying active ingredients and developing multi-faceted implementation strategies. Use the provided excerpt on leadership support during initial implementation.
5. Plan for regular reviews to assess if the plan needs updating.
6. Plan for sustainability of the plan in the future
7. There are several implementation challenges such as ****(add your own challenges)

You can alter the word count accordingly and include any other contextual issues that you want to include in your plan.

Because of scheme/programme copyright, I omitted these for my prompt to enable me to copy the output from Claude. I specified only recognised approaches. Your implementation plan will be much more detailed and informed.

The next step is to cut and paste this into the implementation plan format, BUT ONLY AFTER YOU HAVE CHECKED THE CONTENTS for any "HALLUCINATIONS" which we will address in chapter 11.

Output from Claude would be similar to the following which I then dropped into the EEF planning template:

Here is a Claude-generated 2500-word implementation plan to address the oral language goals at Cherry Tree Lane Primary School:

Claude's response:

Executive Summary

This plan provides a strategic framework to accelerate student growth in vocabulary, listening comprehension, verbal expression, and meaningful interactions. It centres professional learning, schoolwide initiatives, targeted interventions, tracking systems, and community engagement to build critical oral language skills as a foundation for academic success.

Overarching Theme: Bridging the Oral Language Gap

The Problem

Students

- 60% of EYFS pupils enter with below expected oral language levels

- Persistent vocabulary gap through KS2, disproportionately affecting disadvantaged students

- 25% have identified speech/language needs requiring support

Staff

- Variable skills and confidence in teaching oral language across subjects

- Need deeper understanding of language development trajectories

- Require tools to identify needs and track progress

Student Outcomes

- Reading, writing, and curriculum comprehension impacted by insufficient language skills

- KS1/2 results lag national averages, particularly for disadvantaged pupils

Intervention Description

- Establish Schoolwide Focus on Oral Language Development

Active ingredients: committed leadership, dedicated oral language lead teacher, ongoing CPD, language/vocabulary policies.

A cultural shift is required to elevate oral language as a priority across the school. The headteacher and senior leaders will spearhead this focus, dedicating resources and providing strategic direction. An oral language lead teacher will guide implementation, supported by an oral language working group. All staff will receive ongoing professional development to build skills, knowledge, and confidence. School policies will formalise expectations around vocabulary, academic talk, and student discussions.

Research shows committed leadership and a whole-school focus is essential for successful language initiatives (Dockrell et al., 2017).

- Build Staff Capacity Through Tailored Professional Learning

Active ingredients: needs-based workshops, expert training, peer collaboration, reflection on impact.

EYFS staff and language support assistants will receive specialised training on speech/language development, identification of needs, and effective interventions. All teachers will take part in workshops focused on integrating oral language across subjects through explicit vocabulary instruction, rich student talk, and curriculum discussions. Sessions will provide research insights, videos of strategies in action, planning time, and peer collaboration. Follow-up will encourage reflection on student impact.

- High-quality, sustained professional development is linked to successful implementation of oral language initiatives (Murphy et al., 2017).*

- Launch Targeted Oral Language Interventions

Active ingredients: robust identification, small group and 1:1 instruction, engaging resources, ongoing progress monitoring.

Screenings will identify students requiring extra support. Interventions will include tailored small group and 1:1 instruction targeting vocabulary, narrative skills, listening comprehension, and verbal expression. Interactive games, multimedia, and high-interest books will be used. Flexible grouping will allow adjustment based on progress monitoring. Interventions will align with classroom learning.

Research shows interventions using engaging activities delivered with fidelity by trained staff have significant impact on language skills (Bowyer-Crane et al., 2008).

- Increase Quality Student Interactions

Active ingredients: schoolwide initiatives, discussion models, conversation prompts, partner work

Daily activities such as partner sharing, small group discussions, and whole-class conversations will increase meaningful talk. Teachers will utilise models like accountable talk stems and reciprocal teaching to scaffold academic conversations. Open-ended questioning and "think-aloud" activities will be integrated across subjects to build verbal expression.

Oral language skills develop through practice. High-quality interactions expand vocabulary and build verbal fluency (Fisher et al., 2008).*

Launch Tracking and Progress Monitoring

Active ingredients: initial screenings, vocabulary assessments, ongoing monitoring, data review cycles, flagging needs.

Robust tracking will allow close monitoring of language growth. EYFS students will be screened on entry. Curriculum-based vocabulary assessments will track progress by year group. Data cycles will review progress, flag needs, and adjust interventions. Information will be shared with teachers and parents.

Regular monitoring allows responsive adjustment of instruction and early identification of struggling students (Kim et al., 2013).*

Engage Parents as Partners

Active ingredients: workshops, home activities, guidance videos, parent–child reading, communication.

Parent workshops will share oral language development information and simple home strategies like conversational turn-taking, reading aloud, singing, and vocabulary games. Online videos and resources will reinforce workshop content. Families will be encouraged to read together daily. Student progress will be regularly communicated.

Equipping parents with practical strategies to build oral language through daily interactions can significantly accelerate skills (Niklas et al., 2016).

-Implementation Activities

Leadership

- Establish oral language working party to drive initiative and model expectations (Murphy et al., 2017)

- Perform needs analysis through student assessment data, staff surveys, and QA to identify focus areas and goals

- Allocate resources and time for professional development, interventions, assessments, and tracking

- Create schoolwide policies and vision statements around building student oral language

Professional Learning

- Audit staff skills and confidence in teaching oral language through questionnaire (Gillentine, 2006)

- Tailor CPD workshops to needs e.g. EYFS staff training on development norms, interventions, identification; subject teacher sessions on vocabulary and academic talk strategies (Murphy et al., 2017)

- Include active learning, videos, planning time, expert input, and peer collaboration (Darling-Hammond et al., 2017)

- Provide ongoing coaching, modelling, and drop-in support for teachers implementing new strategies. Encourage reflective practice.

Interventions

- Use standardised screenings and vocabulary assessments to identify students requiring extra support (Kim et al., 2013)

- Group students by ability for small group interventions targeting vocabulary, listening comprehension, narrative skills. Reassess every six weeks.

- Invest in engaging, multimedia intervention resources. Provide quiet spaces conducive to language development.

- Ensure trained staff deliver interventions consistently. Monitor fidelity through observations. Adjust groupings based on progress.

Meaningful Interactions

- Roll out schoolwide initiatives like partner-sharing and small group discussions daily (Fisher et al., 2008)

- Model and display conversation stems, accountable talk grids, think-pair-share structures etc

- Set expectations for open-ended questioning and discussions in all subjects

- Use role play, drama, debates to increase verbal rehearsal (Fisher et al., 2008)

Assessment & Tracking

- Establish robust entry assessment for EYFS students using standardised language screenings

- Implement vocabulary knowledge assessments every term to track progress. Analyse gaps.

- Perform ongoing monitoring through small group observations, discussions, and comprehension checks (Kim et al., 2013)

- Review data cycles every six weeks. Plan interventions and groupings accordingly

- Share key data and progress updates with staff and parents regularly

Parental Engagement

- Launch parent oral language workshops focused on research insights and home strategies (Niklas et al., 2016)

- Provide online resources like video tutorials modelling effective techniques

- Encourage parent–child reading through school book bags and reading challenges

- Maintain ongoing communication about child's progress and next steps

Implementation Outcomes

Short Term (Year 1)

- 90% of staff report improved confidence in teaching oral language strategies (PD questionnaire)

- Entry and vocabulary assessments established for all year groups

- Screening identifies 50% of EYFS students requiring targeted interventions

- 30% improvement in vocabulary skills among pupils receiving interventions (assessed termly)

Medium Term (Year 2–3)

- 75%+ lessons demonstrate use of vocabulary and discussion strategies (lesson observations)

- 70% of EYFS/KS1 pupils reach expected oral language levels for age (entry and termly assessments)

- Reading comprehension improves 10% across KS2 (benchmark assessments)

Long Term (Year 4–6)

- 100% pupils at or above age expected oral language levels by Year 6 (entry and termly assessments)

- No significant oral language attainment gaps between disadvantaged pupils and peers (assessment analysis)

- 75%+ pupils achieve expected standard in reading and writing at end of KS2, in line with national average (KS2 results)

Expected Impact

This strategic focus on accelerating the development of oral language skills will close vocabulary gaps, increase student academic discussions, and establish a culture of language-rich interactions across Cherry Tree Lane. As a result, disadvantaged students will have the necessary language foundations to access curriculum content, express themselves clearly, and achieve academic success alongside peers. Robust tracking will enable targeted, responsive interventions based on data. Overall, implementation will provide students with the vocabulary, verbal reasoning, and listening abilities to thrive at school and life.

Regular Reviews

- Termly review of interventions, groupings, and progress data

- Annual review of staff professional development needs

- Yearly audit of tracking systems and assessments

- Ongoing review of vocabulary use and discussion quality through lesson observations

Sustainability

- Maintain oral language lead teacher role to guide continuity

- Enable staff collaboration and informal peer support

- Induct new staff through CPD workshops and mentoring

- Review policies and approaches regularly to keep strategies fresh

- Fund the ongoing purchase of intervention resources

- Maintain tracking systems and robust data cycles

Challenges

- Maintaining staff motivation and consistency long-term

- Providing targeted interventions with limited resources

- Avoiding language assessment fatigue

- Engaging all parents including hard-to-reach families

Top Tip

If a specific approach interests you, ask Claude to provide further information and detail for clarity.

To create the following two examples, I simply copied and pasted from this information while checking, editing, and making specific changes for my fictional school. Going through a quality assurance process from what Claude generates still allows you to produce bespoke plans, as you are the decision maker, selecting aspects or excerpts or full sections of text as you feel appropriate. From Claude's output this is just one example of how a leader may compose an implementation plan.

Please remember that I have not knowingly included systems or approaches that are copyrighted.

Example 1

Overarching Theme: **To equip all stakeholders to build a supportive language environment that closes vocabulary and oracy gaps and elevates literacy and learning.**				
Problem (Why?)	**Intervention Description (What?) Active Ingredients**	**Implementation Activities (How?)**	**Implementation Outcomes short, medium and long term (How well?)**	**Final outcomes (And so?)**
Students: Significant gaps in oral language and vocabulary exist, especially for disadvantaged students. Skills lag well below expectations. **Staff:** Inconsistent teaching approaches Limited staff training. Lack of robust tracking restricts ability to improve students' oral and vocabulary skills effectively. **Outcomes:** Underdeveloped language skills contribute to low attainment across subjects. Stagnating progress in reading, writing, and curriculum subjects	**1.Early Years Enhanced Language Curriculum** A new communication-focused nursery curriculum to build foundational interaction skills through talk, songs, rhyme stories, and play **Active ingredients:** Training in modelled expanded talk, rhymes, vocabulary strategies, collecting and using language data. **2.Staff Training Programme** Comprehensive professional development will equip staff with strategies to develop students' oral language and vocabulary. Training will build expertise in interactions, modelling, effective questioning, vocabulary instruction, SLCN support and using language data to inform teaching. **Active ingredients:** Use of expert trainers, peer observation, reference guides with models **3.Robust Assessment and Tracking** Standardised assessments at baseline and termly intervals will identify language skill gaps. Ongoing monitoring will track all students' progress Active ingredients: Selecting appropriate assessments, staff training in administering and analysing language data **4.Targeted Language Interventions** Small groups and 1:1 session will boost skills for students significantly below expectations. Tailored interventions will utilise repetition, multimedia, narrative, tiered vocabulary, etc **Active ingredients:** Staff training in targeted intervention delivery, planning personalised sessions, applying learnings from data **5.Embedding Language Development** All core & foundation subjects will integrate vocabulary instruction, open-ended talk, and rich language exposure through word banks, discussions, and oral tasks **Active ingredients:** Models for subject leads on embedding language development, shared resource bank **6.Parent Workshops and Home Plans** Workshops and take-home guides will equip parents with practical strategies to improve communication and vocabulary at home **Active ingredients:** Creating accessible parent guidance, training staff in effective workshop delivery.	1. Senior leaders will communicate strategic importance of oral language across improvement plans and internal messaging (EEF). 2. English lead and EYFS lead will audit the nursery curriculum and lead redesign informed by language nutrition approaches (Suskind et al. 2020). 3. EYFS lead will coordinate purchasing of rhymes, stories, and play resources to surround children with rich language. 4. Staff working group will plan CPD on language modelling, interaction strategies, vocabulary development, SLCN support etc., informed by research on impact of teacher training in this area (Starling et al. 2021). 5. English lead and SENCO will select standardised assessments and oversee staff training in administration and analysis. 6. SLT will schedule protected time for small group and 1:1 intervention session. 7. Subject leads will audit existing schemes of work and collaborate to integrate more vocabulary instruction, oral tasks, and open-ended talk across subjects (Flynn, 2016). 8. Parental engagement lead will design workshop content and print take-home guidance around language facilitation strategies for each year group, co-creating with parent focus groups (Toub et al. 2018). 9. Staff will record observations and reflections on new strategies in learning logs, to be discussed in peer coaching.	Short Term (6 months): All staff have completed training on language modelling. F1 curriculum audited and redesigned. Resources purchased. Staff working group established Assessment exploration concluded and selected. 75% of EYFS at age-expected communication levels (from 60%) Baseline assessments established: 60% staff confident in using data. 4 parent workshops delivered; 40% of nursery parents attended. Medium Term (12 months): 1 to 1 intervention established. Subject leaders have re-evaluated curriculums. 90% EYFS at age-expected oral language (from 75%) Interventions allocated for 50% of Years. 1-2 students below standards 8 workshops delivered; 60% parents attended. 70% staff report improved confidence in language teaching.	EYFS oral language gap fully closed. Reading attainment rises from 65% to 80% meeting standard at end of KS1; from 70% to 90% by end of KS2. 90% staff consistently implementing language strategies. Parent surveys show significantly increased language interactions at home. School community has successfully built students' oral and vocabulary skills effectively. Targeted support tackles gaps early while integrated approaches elevate language ability long-term. Students gain strong foundations to excel across the curriculum, reflected in rising outcomes and engagement.

Example 2

Overarching Theme: **To equip all stakeholders to build a supportive language environment that closes vocabulary and oracy gaps and elevates literacy and learning.**				
Problem (Why?)	**Intervention Description (What?) Active Ingredients**	**Implementation Activities (How?)**	**Implementation Outcomes short, medium and long term (How well?)**	**Final outcomes (And so?)**
Students: Significant gaps in oral language and vocabulary exist, especially for disadvantaged students. Skills lag well below expectations. **Staff:** Inconsistent teaching approaches Limited staff training. Lack of robust tracking restricts ability to improve students' oral and vocabulary skills effectively. **Outcomes:** Underdeveloped language skills contribute to low attainment across subjects. Stagnating progress in reading, writing, and curriculum subjects	**1.Early Years Enhanced Language Curriculum** A new communication-focused nursery curriculum to build foundational interaction skills through talk, songs, rhyme stories, and play **Active ingredients:** Training in modelled expanded talk, rhymes, vocabulary strategies, collecting and using language data. **2.Staff Training Programme** Comprehensive professional development will equip staff with strategies to develop students' oral language and vocabulary. Training will build expertise in interactions, modelling, effective questioning, vocabulary instruction, SLCN support and using language data to inform teaching. **Active ingredients:** Use of expert trainers, peer observation, reference guides with models **3.Robust Assessment and Tracking** Standardised assessments at baseline and termly intervals will identify language skill gaps. Ongoing monitoring will track all students' progress Active ingredients: Selecting appropriate assessments, staff training in administering and analysing language data **4.Targeted Language Interventions** Small groups and 1:1 session will boost skills for students significantly below expectations. Tailored interventions will utilise repetition, multimedia, narrative, tiered vocabulary, etc **Active ingredients:** Staff training in targeted intervention delivery, planning personalised sessions, applying learnings from data **5.Embedding Language Development** All core & foundation subjects will integrate vocabulary instruction, open-ended talk, and rich language exposure through word banks, discussions, and oral tasks **Active ingredients:** Models for subject leads on embedding language development, shared resource bank **6.Parent Workshops and Home Plans** Workshops and take-home guides will equip parents with practical strategies to improve communication and vocabulary at home **Active ingredients:** Creating accessible parent guidance, training staff in effective workshop delivery.	1. Senior leaders will communicate strategic importance of oral language across improvement plans and internal messaging (EEF). 2. English lead and EYFS lead will audit the nursery curriculum and lead redesign informed by language nutrition approaches (Suskind et al. 2020). 3. EYFS lead will coordinate purchasing of rhymes, stories, and play resources to surround children with rich language. 4. Staff working group will plan CPD on language modelling, interaction strategies, vocabulary development, SLCN support etc., informed by research on impact of teacher training in this area (Starling et al. 2021). 5. English lead and SENCO will select standardised assessments and oversee staff training in administration and analysis. 6. SLT will schedule protected time for small group and 1:1 intervention session. 7. Subject leads will audit existing schemes of work and collaborate to integrate more vocabulary instruction, oral tasks, and open-ended talk across subjects (Flynn, 2016). 8. Parental engagement lead will design workshop content and print take-home guidance around language facilitation strategies for each year group, co-creating with parent focus groups (Toub et al. 2018). 9. Staff will record observations and reflections on new strategies in learning logs, to be discussed in peer coaching.	Short Term (6 months): All staff have completed training on language modelling. F1 curriculum audited and redesigned. Resources purchased. Staff working group established Assessment exploration concluded and selected. 75% of EYFS at age-expected communication levels (from 60%) Baseline assessments established: 60% staff confident in using data. 4 parent workshops delivered; 40% of nursery parents attended. Medium Term (12 months): 1 to 1 intervention established. Subject leaders have re-evaluated curriculums. 90% EYFS at age-expected oral language (from 75%) Interventions allocated for 50% of Years. 1-2 students below standards 8 workshops delivered; 60% parents attended. 70% staff report improved confidence in language teaching.	EYFS oral language gap fully closed. Reading attainment rises from 65% to 80% meeting standard at end of KS1; from 70% to 90% by end of KS2. 90% staff consistently implementing language strategies. Parent surveys show significantly increased language interactions at home. School community has successfully built students' oral and vocabulary skills effectively. Targeted support tackles gaps early while integrated approaches elevate language ability long-term. Students gain strong foundations to excel across the curriculum, reflected in rising outcomes and engagement.

Chapter 4

Flawless Delivery - Ensure Smooth Rollout and Rapid Results

Now you have created your implementation plan, we can use the delivery prompt to create a draft delivery plan that you can edit.

Please include staff names and as much contextual information to make the plan as close to your requirements as possible.

Your Prompt 9 - Type the following into Claude's chat box:

*Act as an expert in **Education Implementation Plan Delivery Expert** in an English Primary/Secondary school. The output should be **comprehensive delivery plan of 2000 words** for the implementation plan.

Place the focus of your implementation plan here.

The output format should include//A delivery plan may outline components like:

September – Initial training workshops for all staff

October – Peer observations and debriefs.

November – Specialist instructor modelling in classrooms

December – Review feedback, provide additional coaching.

*Rollout timeline over the year from September 20** to August 20**

*Responsible parties – John Smith (EYFS lead) and Jane Dickens (KS1 lead) will lead on this plan

*Resource (Time: 15 mins of staff meeting time over 40 weeks, 4 twilights totalling 8 hours, 2 days of release time for teaching assistants in term time. Budget allocation £5000)

The plan should//

- Provide high quality face-to-face professional development and training to build staff skills in delivering the new approaches using expert trainers where possible

- Offer opportunities for staff to observe strong practice and have expert colleagues model the new strategies, allowing staff to see the approaches in action

- Introduce new practices gradually, so staff can integrate them into their day-to-day teaching in a manageable way that does not overload staff

- Provide ongoing expert coaching and feedback to support staff as they work to embed the new techniques, and encourage reflective discussion to reinforce the learning

- Monitor how well the implementation is going and gather feedback to identify issues early

- Be ready to offer additional support and training to address any gaps

- Allow time for staff to reflect on and refine their use of the new strategies recognising that iteration leads to mastery

- Recognise staff effort and celebrate successes during the intensive delivery phase to maintain motivation and momentum

- Continually emphasise how the new approaches support key school goals to foster staff buy-in. **Make the relevance clear by referencing appropriate research.**

- Use clearly understood UK English

Top Tip

I strongly recommend that the draft plan is generated and reviewed by a senior leadership team. Claude should act as an assistant to your delegated team, not encourage you to work in isolation. It also means that the team get used to prompting as a collective.

Example of draft delivery plan generated by Claude AI:

Enhanced Language and Communication Strategy Delivery Plan

September 20**

- Initial training workshop for all teaching staff during INSET days at the start of the academic year. The two-hour session will introduce the research rationale, expected outcomes, and outline the new strategies to be embedded across the school over the coming year. It will be led by the headteacher, English lead, EYFS lead, and SENCO.

- English and EYFS leads will conduct an audit of current nursery curriculum, schemes of work, and resources to identify areas for enhancement and purchase new materials needed for the enhanced provision.

- SLT will review timetables and allocate protected time slots for small group and 1:1 interventions from October half term onwards.

October 20**

- Specialist external trainer (Speech and Language) will deliver two twilight CPD sessions modelling best practice in language and vocabulary development. The first will focus on strategies for EYFS and KS1 staff, the second for KS2. The twilights will equip staff with practical techniques to apply in their teaching, allow them to plan how they will implement the strategies in their context, and give them opportunities to practise the new approaches.

- English lead will coordinate peer observations so each member of staff can observe at least one modelling session delivered by the specialist trainer in a colleague's classroom. This will build understanding of the new techniques in a real-world context.

- Baseline assessments will be conducted for all nursery and reception pupils using selected standardised tools. SENCO and assessment coordinator will analyse results and identify students requiring targeted interventions.

November 20**

- Peer observations continue, with teachers observing modelled sessions by the specialist trainer across EYFS, KS1 and KS2. Staff will then share reflections in brief coaching sessions afterwards to support integration of the new strategies into daily practice.

- EYFS lead will pilot a parent workshop for nursery parents, gathering feedback to refine the one-hour session on using language facilitation techniques at home. Take-home guidance documents will be evaluated by attendees.

December 20**

- Second specialist external trainer workshop for all staff will enable teachers to share their experience with implementation so far, thereby providing feedback and gaining solutions to any challenges faced. The trainer will advise on refinement of approaches and respond to all staff questions.

- Assessment coordinator will retest a sample of pupils using the baseline language assessments to review early progress and allow further adjustment of interventions if required.

January 20**

- SENCO begins first wave of tailored small group and 1:1 interventions for pupils identified through baseline data as needing additional support. Interventions will take place during the allocated slots, following tailored plans coordinated by SENCO and delivered by trained TAs.

-EYFS lead rolls out refined parent workshops to all nursery families, aiming for at least 50% of parents to attend. KS1 lead pilot workshops with reception parents.

February 20**

- Subject leads from across the curriculum will collaborate in working groups half a day per week during this month to audit current schemes of work. They will enhance all units of work to intentionally integrate more planned opportunities for open-ended talk, rich vocabulary exposure, and discussion tasks across all subject areas.

March 20**

- English lead delivers refresher training at staff meeting, recapping core language development strategies, providing guidance documents detailing the approaches, and sharing updated schemes of work.

- KS1 lead rolls out parent workshops to families across Years 1–2, supported by class teachers.

April 20****

- Assessment coordinator analyses data from standardised language assessments for EYFS pupils to review progress after two terms and adjust interventions as required.

May 20****

- Peer review of enhanced schemes of work by subject leads, gathering final feedback from teachers on integrating language-rich strategies into all subject plans.

- Parental engagement lead sends parental survey to gain feedback on workshops, take-home materials, and understand observed progress in children's communication at home.

June 20****

- Repeat specialist external trainer workshop enables all staff to share progress, troubleshoot any final challenges, and celebrate successes in enhancing language provision. Trainer emphasises sustaining changes achieved.

July 20****

- INSET training led by English lead recaps the programme, shares parental survey outcomes, highlighting positive shifts, and discusses next steps for further enhancement in new academic year.

- Final analysis of pupil language assessment data by assessment coordinator and SENCO shows impact on attainment.

- Senior leadership team meet to review feedback, assess outcomes achieved, plan any continued support needed, and communicate next phase developments to all staff, pupils, and parents. Celebrate successes!

Chapter 5

Sustain Positive Momentum – Make Your Plan Stick for the Long Haul

Now we can do the same for a sustainability plan.

Prompt 10 – Type the following into Claude's chat box:

* Act as an expert **Sustainability Plan Generator*** Your output should be a **sustainability plan of 2000 words** to support the implementation plan for an English primary/secondary school on:

Place the focus of your Implementation pla

Use UK English and phrasing which should be clearly understood. The output format should include:

- Planning for sustaining and scaling the implementation from the very beginning – build sustainability into the initial design

- To sustain momentum, continually reconnect goals to school values. For example, "Elevating teaching practices aligns with our mission of fostering lifelong learners".

- Respond quickly to any erosion of fidelity through additional training and support

- Provide ongoing professional development and expert support so staff continue refining skills. Don't halt capacity building.

- Enable staff collaboration time to share best practices and problem-solve together. Peer support fuels sustainability.

- Recognise staff contributions and celebrate successes to maintain enthusiasm.

- Monitor implementation fidelity and adapt supports based on data. Address any erosion quickly.

- Embed the approaches into policies, systems, and induction processes. Integrate them into "how we do things here".

- Plan for staff turnover by training new teachers and leaders

- Review costs associated with the approaches and make plans for ongoing funding allocation

- consider sustainability of the initiative

- Continually gather feedback from staff and students to drive continuous refinement and adaptation

- Share positive implementation outcomes with all stakeholders to highlight impact

Chapter 6

Precision Tracking – Monitor, Evaluate, and Continuously Improve

Your Prompt 11 – Type the following into Claude's chat box:

> *** Act as an expert in school monitoring and evaluation***Your objective is to***Develop a comprehensive M&E plan for the implementation plan***The professional adults in a school are the audience* The plan will focus on:
>
> ➡ Place the focus of your Implementation plan here
>
> The monitoring and evaluation plan output should:
>
> - Establish a monitoring system early in the process to track progress and identify issues requiring support
>
> - Take baseline measurements before implementation to support comparison later
>
> - Use a combination of quantitative data (e.g., assessments) and qualitative feedback (e.g., interviews) for well-rounded understanding, whichever is relevant to the plan.

- Ensure monitoring implementation fidelity – ensuring that implementation is being delivered as intended

- Gather staff perceptions on facilitators/barriers to inform adaptions and iterations

- Review multiple indicators related to implementation goals – and not rely on just one data source

- Schedule regular check-ins to review data and assess what's working/not working

- Allow adapting support based on monitoring data to optimise implementation quality.

- Consider and suggest short-term indicators and longer-term impact.

- Specifically measure impact of the development theme.

- Use expertise such as researchers/evaluators to support objective data analysis

- Plan ahead for how monitoring data will be used for improvement during and after implementation

- Communicate and report on monitoring findings to sustain stakeholder engagement

- Balance pragmatic data collection which minimises staff workload

And that's a wrap! Your implementation plans and plans for monitoring and evaluation, delivery, and sustainability are ready to be checked and tweaked to meet your needs and the context of your school. I hope these prompts speed up your planning process whether a subject leader or senior leader and I hope you are now ready to change the prompts that are generalised to be more specific to your needs and context.

The next part of the handbook is for you to find out a little more about artificial intelligence.

Part 2

Deepening Your Knowledge and Understanding of AI

Chapter 7

Understanding AI as a Tool to Enhance Education – Maximise the Benefits, Minimise the Risks

Artificial intelligence, or AI, has become ubiquitous across society. Yet education in England has been slow to leverage its potential, unlike places such as Japan where guidance already exists on integrating AI into lessons and schools with the aim to make young people responsible users and promote AI literacy (4th July 2023) (3)

As a school leader, you may be wondering – what exactly is AI, and how can it augment teaching and learning? This chapter aims to provide a balanced overview of AI's immense possibilities in schools, as well as the ethical challenges leaders face. With prudent guidance, AI has the possibility to become a benevolent aid supporting staff, pupils, and leaders.

The Promise of AI in Education

AI is becoming integral to modern life. Rather than replacing teachers, AI can enhance instruction when thoughtfully implemented. For example, AI can analyse pupil data to personalise learning paths, or automate administrative tasks to optimise teachers' time with pupils.

Realising these benefits relies on the thoughtful integration of AI guided by qualified educators. With proper oversight and care, AI can adapt to each pupil, provide data insights, and maximise human potential for pupils, teachers, and leaders.

Clarifying Misconceptions About AI

A common myth is that AI aims to wholly replace teachers. AI lacks uniquely human strengths – empathy, creativity, wisdom, emotional intelligence, and the ability to gain trust – the things that make great educators.

Many people mistakenly think that AI is perfect and fair, but this is far from the truth. AI systems can be biased by the data they are trained on, which can have negative consequences for those using it. That's why we need to ensure that AI is developed and deployed with proper oversight and regulation, so that we can address the potential risks around transparency, security, privacy, and ethics in a responsible way. This is also the main message of a great blog post by Ethan Mollick (4), who reminds us that AI is not a magic solution for everything. AI has its own limitations and drawbacks, and sometimes it may not be the best tool for the job. Before using AI for any purpose, we should carefully consider whether it can handle the task effectively and ethically, given its weaknesses.

While excellent at specialised tasks like data analysis, AI still lacks general human intelligence and emotional capabilities. As Emad Mostaque, CEO of Stability AI said in 2023:

"AI will not replace humans, humans using AI will replace humans"(6)

For the foreseeable future, human stewardship remains essential to direct AI's development ethically.

AI is a tool complementing human strengths like critical thinking, and the ability to build meaningful connections with students. With proper oversight, AI can augment these uniquely human skills and capacities within education.

In "The Future of AI in Education: 13 Things We Can Do to Minimize the Damage" Arran Hamilton (Cognition Learning Group) Dylan Wiliam (University College London) John Hattie (University of Melbourne) 8 August 2023"(5) appeared this helpful overview of some of the promising applications as well as risks involved with integrating AI technologies in educational settings. As the authors emphasise, we need to carefully consider both the upsides and downsides to make informed choices about if, when, and how these tools should be utilised to truly benefit students rather than potentially causing harm. Ongoing ethical scrutiny, transparency, evidence-based implementation, and teacher involvement will be critical to maximising the advantages while minimising the dangers.

Benefits	Concerns
Scaling quality education in hard to reach contexts; greater personalization; adaptive content; democratization of access; reductions in the cost of educational service delivery; teacher workload reductions; culturally relevant content; continuous assessment and feedback; coaching systems that help us to maintain goal commitment; decision support systems that help educational institutions to develop 'good' plans and stick to them; AI digital tutors instead of expensive high-intensity human tuition for learners with additional needs; AI support to teachers through augmented reality heads-up displays; deeper inferences about student learning through bio feedback tracking; faster identification and support for neuro-diverse learners; and multi-modal access for children with disabilities.	Accuracy (producing confident but incorrect answers); content bias; data protection, privacy and protection; plagiarism; surveillance of students and teachers; systems using poor pedagogic reasoning to increase pace of instruction for some students and to reduce it for others; equity of outcomes; algorithmic discrimination – where systems are used to make enrolment decisions/identify students for additional support; AI systems and tools that make decisions where it is impossible to understand how they are made; and worries that AI models take little account of context, and are focused on shallow factual knowledge.

Source: author adaptation from US Department for Education Office of Educational Technology (2023); UNESCO (2021, 2022 & 2023); Giannini, (2023).

The DfE's Stance on AI in Education

In March 2023, the DfE released a statement titled "Generative artificial intelligence in education"(7) aligning with this chapter's themes that AI offers opportunities, but oversight is crucial. It advised preventing misconduct, upholding integrity and privacy, monitoring risks, and sharing best practices. This stance acknowledges benefits while cautioning against overreliance, as AI cannot replace qualified teachers.

As an education leader embracing AI's potential while remaining mindful of limitations, you are well positioned to incorporate its benefits prudently. With an eye towards developing critical thinking and mastery, and upholding quality, integrity, privacy and safeguarding, leaders can obtain the best of both human and machine.

Chapter 8

Prime your AI Assistant for Success – Upgrade Knowledge in Your Domain

Priming and prompting are two different ways of providing an AI assistant like Claude with extra context or direction when having a conversation. Here's a quick breakdown of how they differ:

Priming involves giving the AI background information or a frame of reference before a conversation starts, to help steer the dialogue in a particular direction. For example, a researcher could prime Claude by explaining the topic they want to discuss or providing relevant documents to read ahead of time. This allows AI to have existing knowledge to draw on when conversing.

Prompting happens during a conversation, when a human provides additional details to focus AI responses or steer the dialogue. For instance, if you were talking about holiday plans, you might prompt with "How about someplace warm?" This gives a specific criterion to consider when making suggestions. Prompts keep AI on topic and guide the conversation in real time.

The key difference is that:

Priming happens beforehand to give context, while…

Prompting happens in line to steer the ongoing dialogue.

Both are useful techniques for having more productive conversations with an AI.

Priming is like giving AI a homework assignment to read about a topic before we talk about it. So, if you are going to discuss holiday plans, you might have AI read some travel guides first. This gets AI ready for the conversation.

The main difference is that priming prepares AI with background info before a chat. Prompting guides AI during the conversation to maintain its focus. Priming is like studying, while prompting is like getting helpful hints! Both make AI better at conversing and understanding what you want to talk about.

As an AI assistant, Claude does not have independent access to browse websites or databases. However, a key benefit is that you can directly provide relevant documents to augment Claude's knowledge.

Here is a brief guide:

1. Identify documents with valuable insights like reports, briefings, research papers, or presentations

2. Download or save the files locally so they are accessible

3. In a chat conversation, use the attach file option to upload the document

4. Offer specific guidance on what to focus on from the material

(A more detailed step-by-step guide is included later in this chapter.)

Given the limitations of our chat interface, Claude can only process attachments of up to 150MB in size. For larger files, they need to be uploaded in sections.

Some tips to condense size while preserving quality:

- Use optimisation tools for PDFs

- Compress image resolution or formats

- Remove unnecessary formatting/pages

- Split into multiple smaller attachments if needed

Providing focused, concise information allows Claude to work most effectively.

A major benefit is that Claude can "remember" documents you previously provided and reference them in future discussions, without you needing to continuously re-upload. Simply indicate you are referring to a specific document from chat history and Claude can incorporate those insights.

For example, if you previously shared a research paper, you could later prompt:

"Based on the findings from the research on [topic] I previously shared, please summarise implementation recommendations..."

Quick context helps refresh Claude's memory, as well as build on our shared knowledge.

So, let's try it together.

Whether secondary, primary or special leader we all must address our pupil premium strategy in the first term of any school's year.

In March 2023 the DfE updated pupil premium guidance for schools.

It can be located here:

https://assets.publishing.service.gov.uk/government/uploads/system/uploads/attachment_data/file/1147853/Using_pupil_premium_guidance_for_school_leaders.pdf (8)

Here is a step-by-step guide to downloading the pupil premium guidance document to share with Claude:

Step 1) Identify that the document you want Claude to access is the pupil premium guidance. This contains relevant information about pupil premium policies that you want Claude to review.

Step 2) Use a search engine or go to the Department for Education website to locate the pupil premium guidance document.

Step 3) Once on the pupil premium guidance page, check for a download button or link to save a copy of the document.

Step 4) If a clear download option is not present, look for a print option and choose to print/save as a PDF file. This will generate a PDF copy of the guidance.

Step 5) When prompted, choose to download the PDF version of the pupil premium guidance document to your computer. Take note of which folder you save it to.

Step 6) As this is a lengthy document, consider downloading it by chapter or section for easier processing. Look for options to download by part.

Step 7) After downloading the pupil premium guidance fully or partially, open your chat with Claude.

Step 8) Click the "attach file paperclip" icon and navigate to the folder where you saved the pupil premium guidance PDF.

Step 9) Select the pupil premium guidance file and upload it to Claude via the chat.

Step 10) Once uploaded, Claude will be able to access and analyse the pupil premium guidance contents.

Step 11) Provide Claude with specific instructions about what information you need from the pupil premium document.

Prompt 12 – Type the following into Claude's chat box:

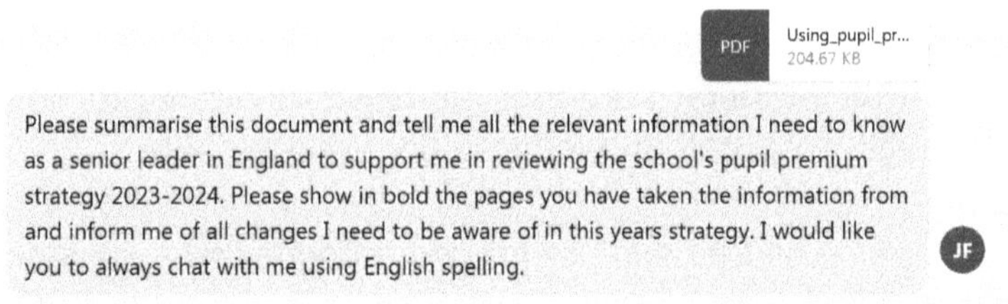

Try out prompt 12 and see what you think to Claude's responses.

Using these as well as documents shots will allow an AI assistant to incorporate information from existing sources rather than just the prompter's assertions. Providing relevant shots can improve an AI's response quality.

(A "shot" is a compact piece of helpful information extracted from a source and injected into a prompt to enhance an AI's knowledge. They help ground AI responses in factual evidence.)

Some best practices around using shots:

- Keep shots concise and focused on the most relevant information. Avoid large blocks of text.

- Use citations and references for transparency

- Provide context on how you want the shot applied

- Summarise or explain shots that may require interpretation

- Use multiple varied shots to get a diversity of perspectives

*I suggest that you select other documents and "shots" to share with Claude that are relevant to the "problem" areas you may be focused upon in your school improvement planning e.g. Oracy, vocabulary, maths or reading. We address this in the next chapter.

Chapter 9

Mastering the Art of Prompting

Prompting is the practice of providing an AI assistant with a carefully crafted prompt to elicit the most relevant, high-quality response. It is an essential skill for successfully leveraging AI. Like any expertise, excellent prompting is developed through continuous iteration and improvement. This chapter provides concrete frameworks, examples, and troubleshooting tips to guide you on the journey towards prompting mastery. Expect an evolution of your abilities with regular practice.

We'll also unpack why prompts may seem less polite than expected, and how unusual syntax enhances effectiveness.

A Note on Prompt Syntax

Readers may have noticed the prompts provided in this book have an unusually direct style, omitting niceties like "please" and "thank you". This stark approach was challenging to me personally at first since politeness is ingrained in me. However, I learned this straightforward syntax helps prompts cut through the noise directly to their objective.

AI systems like Claude do not actually experience gratitude or take offense at bluntness. Flowery language fails to enhance their comprehension – it just introduces superfluous words. Direct, terse phrasing helps focus prompts and reduces ambiguity.

Unconventional punctuation like dashes, asterisks, and brackets also serve a purpose. They help chunk long prompts into digestible sections, clarify desired inputs and outputs, and isolate key parameters. This syntax may seem odd in a book, but it aids prompt precision.

I adapted a matter-of-fact prompting style not out of rudeness, but because concision and clarity enable AI assistants to understand prompts effectively. The unusual syntax many find initially off-putting is designed to enhance human–AI collaboration. Mastering this stripped-down prompting language was crucial to unleash the full power of AI for readers.

With the rationale for direct prompting style explained, let's look at some frameworks for constructing optimised prompts.

Most people use Claude in beginner mode when they first start chatting but with some practice, you can learn how to have great conversations.

Let me share seven tips to help you ask better questions. Then I'll give you a formula to follow and show some examples.

Be Specific: Don't ask vague questions. Give lots of details so Claude knows exactly what information you're looking for.

Say Why You're Asking: If you have a reason for asking, say it. For example, "I'm looking for a dog that is child friendly. What breed would you recommend?"

Use Good Spelling and Grammar: You don't have to be perfect. But try to spell things correctly. This will help Claude understand you better.

Ask for the Type of Answer You Want: Say if you want bullet points, a few sentences, a paragraph explanation etc. This helps Claude tailor a response.

Ask Follow Up Questions:

Try Rephrasing: If one question doesn't work, try asking it a different way.

Ask Claude to Check Facts: You can say "Can you check if this fact is true?" See later chapter on “ÁI Hallucinations”.

Here is a simple formula to follow when you start prompting Claude:

[Context]* + *[Details]* + *[Why You're Asking]* + *[How You Want Me to Answer]

Chapter 10

Troubleshooting Prompts – Refine Your Skills Through Practice

This chapter provides concrete frameworks, examples, and troubleshooting tips to guide you on the journey towards prompting mastery.

The anatomy of an effective prompt – moving the prompt on from the simple formula

This is key to mastering prompting.

Strong prompts act as a roadmap, guiding the AI to the destination of an optimal response. Follow these steps when constructing prompts:

1. **Objective**

State your purpose clearly upfront. E.g., "Summarise key cognitive science research on retrieval practice."

2. Context

Give necessary background details and constraints. E.g., "In the context of a high school history classroom."

3. Specifics

Provide any additional parameters or criteria. E.g., "Focus on studies from the past 5 years involving students ages 14–18."

4. Action

Explain exactly what you want the AI to do. E.g., "Please describe 3–4 key findings from relevant studies."

5. Output

Specify the desired response format. E.g., "Present each study in 2–3 sentences in paragraph form."

6. Optimisation

Refine phrasing to be as clear and simple as possible. Eliminate ambiguity and in UK English.

Prompt Troubleshooting

Pinpointing issues with problematic prompts enables targeted improvements:

- Prompt is too vague: prompt (provide more details on goals, context, constraints).
- AI seems confused: prompt (simplify sentence structure, remove complexity).
- Response lacks depth: prompt (request expanded explanation with examples).
- Information is questionable: prompt (ask AI to cite sources and fact check).

Practice Prompt with Feedback

Initial Prompt: Please suggest some formative assessment strategies.

AI Response: Formative assessment strategies include exit tickets, think-pair-share, student conferences, and observing student work.

Feedback: This prompt is vague. The response lacks context and depth.

Revised Prompt: As a secondary school math teacher, what are 3–4 formative assessment strategies I could use during lessons to check student understanding of quadratic equations? For each, please give a 2–3-sentence example of how it could look in practice.

AI Response: Strategies could include:

- Whiteboard checks – have students work out a quadratic equation example on mini whiteboards and hold up answers to check for understanding.

- Exit slips – at the end of class, have students individually solve a quadratic equation and hand in answers to review.

- Student conferences – sit down with 2–3 students during in-class work time and ask them to walk through solving a quadratic equation while providing feedback.

- Think-pair-share – after introducing quadratic formula, have students work a practice problem individually then discuss with a partner.

This improved prompt provides more specifics for a tailored response with actionable examples.

By following the steps and troubleshooting guide, you will make steady progress in prompting expertise. Remember – your skills will strengthen through regular practice and reflection. Good prompters aren't born overnight. Resilience is needed!

Chapter 11

Verify to Avoid Hallucinations – Validate AI Outputs for Truthfulness

What are AI Hallucinations?

Artificial intelligence systems like Claude do not actually "experience" hallucinations in the same way humans do. They do not have senses or consciousness. However, AIs can sometimes generate text, images, or other content that does not reflect reality. These false outputs are referred to as "AI hallucinations".

AI hallucinations happen when an AI system generates content that seems realistic but is not actually based on real-world facts. For example, an AI image generator could create an image of a fictional person who does not exist. Or an AI text generator could write a news article about an event that never happened.

These imaginary outputs don't come from nowhere – they are created by finding patterns in the AI's training data. AI is trained on many examples of realistic faces; it learns to generate new faces with realistic features. But sometimes those features get mixed and matched in unusual ways, creating faces of people who don't exist.

It's important to note AI's don't intentionally fabricate false outputs. They don't have human motivations like wanting to lie or play make-believe. AI hallucinations are simply artifacts of the statistical learning process. When sampling from a huge space of possibilities, sometimes AI's generate content that passes human judgement as realistic but is not actually grounded in reality.

As AI capabilities advance, researchers are working on ways to improve factual accuracy and reduce hallucinated content. But for now, AI hallucinations remain an occasional occurrence, especially with cutting-edge generative AI systems. The outputs seem impressively realistic but are not always true so for now it remains imperative that you self-validate your work and the research used in your planning. Don’t always take it at face value.

Top Tips – Potential Hallucinations for Educators

Here are some examples of potential "hallucinations" that could occur with AI systems like Claude, and tips for how education staff can identify them:

- The AI generates research findings that sound plausible but are completely made up. For example, claiming "A 2022 study by Smith et al at Oxford University showed personalised tutoring increased maths scores by 70%."

To catch this, staff should verify any key facts/statistics by looking up the original source. Beware studies from vague sources.

- The AI writes an implementation plan that includes references to programmes, curricula, or staff that don't exist at your school. For example, "Ms Anderson from the media studies department will lead teacher training."

Staff should carefully review plans for inaccuracies about their specific school context that reveal the AI's lack of real knowledge.

- When asked for curriculum resources, the AI generates coherent lesson plans on the spot with fictitious sources. For example, "This 10-lesson unit plan on fractions comes from the new 2022 edition of the XYZ Math Curriculum."

Staff should be sceptical of very detailed, polished resources claimed to come from major published curricula. Double check the source.

- The AI provides feedback on students or policies using made-up details. For example, "Student surveys last year showed only 50% satisfaction with the revised lunch options."

Staff should be wary of any detailed data or facts about their school that they didn't provide, as the AI cannot obtain internal information.

Being alert for subtle inaccuracies like these will help staff identify when AI outputs may not be grounded. Checking anything that seems questionable against known facts is key.

There are numerous ways to self-validate information/data using the internet and even asking Claude to fact check.

Type the following into Claude's chat box:

Fact Checking

"Claude, I have a claim that I am unsure about. The claim is [state claim]. As an AI assistant without biases, could you please help me research this claim from reputable sources to determine if it is factual? Summarise the key evidence you find

that supports or refutes this claim. Focus on presenting information from reliable sources in a neutral tone.

Conclusion

Seize the Future Today – Pioneer AI-Accelerated School Improvement

The use of AI technology like Claude for school improvement planning represents an exciting shift that can transform one of the most vital but arduous leadership tasks. The benefits are clear: plans developed with AI are created faster, can be built upon valid research, and provide personalised guidance far surpassing what any individual can offer in the same amount of time.

This book provides a practical roadmap for education leaders to successfully integrate Claude into their planning by sharing lessons learned thus far. However, the learning continues – there may be those who approach this process quite differently. The book demonstrates one model that saves precious time, but prompts can always be moulded to yield better and better results.

The capabilities of AI assistants like Claude will only continue to expand in the coming years. You may consider AI taking on other responsibilities – not just co-developing plans, but potentially helping manage communication, provide real-time data insights, and assist with ongoing monitoring and adaptation. Schools that embrace this technology now will have a head start in leveraging AI to transform education, especially teacher workload.

Using AI allows leaders to spend less time on routine paperwork and compliance. Instead, they can dedicate their energies towards deeper analysis, creative problem-solving, and developing the interpersonal relationships that are the heart of school communities. By embracing AI as a trusted planning partner, schools can make progress while raising the standard of learning for all students.

I hope this handbook provides you with a view into one use of AI in education and I hope that you are inspired to write your own prompts and engage with AI.

References

1. **"Putting Evidence to Work: A School's Guide to Implementation Guidance Report 2019"** https://educationendowmentfoundation.org.uk/education-evidence/guidance-reports/implementation
2. EEF Exemplar Implementation Plans https://d2tic4wvo1iusb.cloudfront.net/production/eef-guidance-reports/implementation/EEF-Example-of-Implementation-Plans.pdf?v=1692705886

3. Kyodo News 4 July 2023, "Japan publishes guidelines allowing limited use of AI in schools."
4. Blog from Ethan Mollick 15 July 2023, "How to use AI to do stuff: An opinionated guide."
5. "The Future of AI in Education: 13 things we can do to minimize the damage", Arran Hamilton (Cognition Learning Group) Dylan Wiliam (University College London) John Hattie (University of Melbourne) 8 August 2023
6. You Tube Video Emad Mostaque, CEO of Stability AI 2023: "AI will not replace humans, humans using AI will replace humans."
7. DfE statement: "Generative artificial intelligence in education."

8. Pupil premium guidance for school leaders

   https://assets.publishing.service.gov.uk/government/uploads/system/uploads/attachment_data/file/1147853/Using_pupil_premium_guidance_for_school_leaders.pdf

Milton Keynes UK
Ingram Content Group UK Ltd.
UKHW020843271023
431440UK00015B/555

9 781916 820739